WELCOME TO THE WRITER'S JOURNAL

A writer's journal is a safe space for you to create, explore, and reflect on your thoughts, feelings, writing sessions, and writing habits, without concern of judgment or criticism.

I'm Alicia-Joy Pierre. I'm a writer, storyteller, and author. I created this journal to share the joy I have found in keeping a writer's journal. It has deepened my writing practice and helped me get clearer on my true voice. I hope it can do the same for you.

The Writer's Journal can serve many purposes:

1. Digging Deeper: It can help you dive deeper into your feelings and thoughts, which in turn helps you to write in alignment with your true voice.

2. Storage: Capture ideas, events, thoughts, poems, powerful images, and notable conversations you overhear (yes, it's okay to eavesdrop at times. This can be a great source of ideas for writing), Writers are observers. This is what we do. We pay careful attention to the inner and outer world and then explore these observations further through written words. Use this journal to store these observations. It's almost impossible to try to remember them all.

3. Warm-Up: Get your creative juices flowing before you start your formal writing. Every day, by the time I finish writing in my journal, I am ready to sit at my computer and go. I am in flow. This didn't come immediately, but through repeated journaling. Consistency matters.

4. Reflection: At the end of the day, I usually take a few minutes to write quick notes about my writing sessions (how I'm feeling about my writing, what I may do differently, etc..).

Structure of this journal (+ suggestions for use):

Part 1: Five pages for you to log your big writing project goals. Whether you're a blogger, aspiring author, article writer, or have any other writing goals, you can use this section to get clear on your writing projects, research needed, and timeframes for project completion.

Plus: Exercises to help you when you're feeling blocked, or not writing regularly.

Part 2: 200 pages of alternating prompts and inspiring writing quotes. You can use the prompts/quotes as inspiration to write, or you can totally ignore them and write what you choose. It's your journal. Use it in the way that serves you best. You have two full pages to write. **If you do not use the full two pages for your morning journaling, I suggest you use the 2nd page (on the right hand side) for your Writing Reflections at the end of the day.**

Part 3: 44 blank pages. You can use these as an overflow from the lined pages. You can also draw, doodle, paste in photos/images, whatever sparks your creativity.

I recommend consistent journaling (for at least 10 minutes a day). Many people find it easiest to journal every morning and then spend a few minutes at the end of the day reflecting on the day and writing about it. Doing this regularly helps build a writing habit.

Keep in mind that you are not editing. Write without filtering. Don't think about grammar, sentence structure, spelling, etc. Just write.

I treasure my writing journal. It has helped me immensely on my creative journey. I hope it can do the same for you.

Alicia-joy
ALICIAJOY.NET

"Exercise the writing muscle every day, even if it is only a letter, notes, a title list, a character sketch, a journal entry. Writers are like dancers, like athletes. Without that exercise, the muscles seize up."
– Jane Yolen

Writing Goals

Whether you write books, blog posts, screenplays, or anything else, you can use this section to record and track your goals. This is especially useful for big writing projects.

PROJECT #1

Start date:

Planned completion date:

Milestones: (For example, outline completed by June 5th, 3,000 words by June 10th, 10,000 words by June 17th, etc.)

Related resources / quotes:

Research needed:

Writing Goals

Whether you write books, blog posts, screenplays, or anything else, you can use this section to record and track your goals. This is especially useful for big writing projects.

PROJECT #2

Start date:

Planned completion date:

Milestones: (For example, outline completed by June 5th, 3,000 words by June 10th, 10,000 words by June 17th, etc.)

Related resources / quotes:

Research needed:

Writing Goals

Whether you write books, blog posts, screenplays, or anything else, you can use this section to record and track your goals. This is especially useful for big writing projects.

PROJECT #3

Start date:

Planned completion date:

Milestones: (For example, outline completed by June 5th, 3,000 words by June 10th, 10,000 words by June 17th, etc.)

Related resources / quotes:

Research needed:

Writing Goals

Whether you write books, blog posts, screenplays, or anything else, you can use this section to record and track your goals. This is especially useful for big writing projects.

PROJECT #4
Start date:
Planned completion date:
Milestones: (For example, outline completed by June 5th, 3,000 words by June 10th, 10,000 words by June 17th, etc.)

Related resources / quotes:

Research needed:

Writing Goals

Whether you write books, blog posts, screenplays, or anything else, you can use this section to record and track your goals. This is especially useful for big writing projects.

PROJECT #5
Start date:
Planned completion date:
Milestones: (For example, outline completed by June 5th, 3,000 words by June 10^{th,} 10,000 words by June 17th, etc.)

Related resources / quotes:

Research needed:

Writing about writing. Exercises to help you when you're feeling blocked, or not writing regularly. If you're stuck on a piece of writing, or struggling to get through it, you can use a month (or week or longer) to focus and write in your journal about the process and difficulties you're having to help you uncover what's blocking you.

Write about writing (as a verb): how does it make you feel to write, what do you most/least like writing, why haven't you been writing as much as you'd like to as of late (if that's the case), what topics (if any) are you afraid to write about?

Write about writing (as the noun): Have you ever read a piece of writing that touched you, shook you to core, released emotions? We all have. Why is that? Why can a page of text or lines on a screen have such an impact? What about the written word do you love most? Is it the imagination it triggers? The relatability? The fact that for a few moments you are immersed in another world? Write about this. You can take it further by thinking about:

*The type(s) of writing you most love to read.

*Who are you favorite authors/writers?

What books/poems inspired you as a child? Why?

What piece of writing most inspired you lately?

Is there someone's writing you adore? Why?

Revisit these questions as often as needed.

Date:

Be a keen observer. Use all of your senses right now and write about the present. What are you seeing/feeling/hearing/smelling? You can choose to write about just one sense or all of them. (this exercise may also help you anytime you are struggling to write or feeling blocked). Keep writing, don't think too much and do not lift the pen off the page. Let one thought lead to another and write, write, write. You'll be surprised what may come up.

Date:

"Words are a lens to focus one's mind."
– Ayn Rand

Date:

Why do you write ? What's the reason for your writing (or wanting to write)?

_____

_____

_____

_____

_____

_____

_____

_____

_____

_____

_____

_____

_____

_____

_____

_____

_____

Date:

"If you have other things in your life—family, friends, good productive day work—these can interact with your writing and the sum will be all the richer."
– David Brin

Date:

What's bothering you about a current creative project or goal that you have? If everything is humming along just fine, write about that.

_____

_____

_____

_____

_____

_____

_____

_____

_____

_____

_____

_____

_____

_____

_____

_____

_____

_____

Date:

"It is perfectly okay to write garbage—as long as you edit brilliantly."
– C. J. Cherryh

Date:

When was the last time you missed a writing goal? Why do you think that happened?

_____

_____

_____

_____

_____

_____

_____

_____

_____

_____

_____

_____

_____

_____

_____

_____

_____

Date:

"A writer without interest or sympathy for the foibles of his fellow man is not conceivable as a writer."
– Joseph Conrad

Date:

When was the most recent time you felt creatively blocked? How did you get over it? If it is now, brainstorm 10 (totally random) ways you can get out of this (some may even seem cheesy, like: go to the movie, eat something delicious). Write more, think less. You never know what ideas may come from this brainstorm.

Date:

"Creativity is an act of defiance."
-Twyla Tharp

Date:

What was the last book you read that you enjoyed? Write a review of
it. What did you most enjoy about it?

_____

_____

_____

_____

_____

_____

_____

_____

_____

_____

_____

_____

_____

_____

_____

_____

_____

Date:

"The scariest moment is always just before you start."
-Stephen King

Date:

What do you see out your window? Describe the view in as much detail as you can.

_____

_____

_____

_____

_____

_____

_____

_____

_____

_____

_____

_____

_____

_____

_____

_____

_____

Date:

"Tears are words that need to be written."
-Paulo Coelho

_____

_____

_____

_____

_____

_____

_____

_____

_____

_____

_____

_____

_____

_____

_____

_____

_____

_____

Date:

What was the last book you read that disappointed you? Why was it
disappointing? If you could directly communicate with the author,
what would you say?

_____

_____

_____

_____

_____

_____

_____

_____

_____

_____

_____

_____

_____

_____

_____

_____

_____

_____

Date:

"Write with the door closed. Rewrite with the door open."
-Stephen King

Date:

Does it make you uncomfortable to sustain eye-contact with strangers (such as on the bus/train/in the grocery store)? Why do you think that is?

Date:

"Get it down. Take chances. It may be bad, but it's the only way you can do anything really good."
– William Faulkner

Date:

Do you have any cravings you'd like to overcome? What triggers these cravings? Can you recall when they first started?

_____

_____

_____

_____

_____

_____

_____

_____

_____

_____

_____

_____

_____

_____

_____

_____

_____

Date:

"Writing is its own reward."
– Henry Miller

_____

_____

_____

_____

_____

_____

_____

_____

_____

_____

_____

_____

_____

_____

_____

_____

_____

_____

Date:

Write about a piece of jewelry you have. Describe it. Where did you get it? How do you feel when you wear it? Do you feel any different with/without wearing it?

_____

_____

_____

_____

_____

_____

_____

_____

_____

_____

_____

_____

_____

_____

_____

_____

_____

Date:

"You can fix anything but a blank page."
-Nora Roberts

Date:

Write about a recent argument/conflict you had. How did it end? How could it have ended differently?

_____

_____

_____

_____

_____

_____

_____

_____

_____

_____

_____

_____

_____

_____

_____

_____

Date:

"You can't wait for inspiration, you have to go after it with a club."
-Jack London

Date:

Imagine you are inside of an old, abandoned house. How do you feel? What's there?

_____

_____

_____

_____

_____

_____

_____

_____

_____

_____

_____

_____

_____

_____

_____

_____

Date:

"No one can write decently who is distrustful of the reader's intelligence or whose attitude is patronizing."
– E. B. White

Date:

It really bothers me when people...........

_____

_____

_____

_____

_____

_____

_____

_____

_____

_____

_____

_____

_____

_____

_____

_____

_____

_____

Date:

"Great is the art of beginning, but greater is the art of ending."
– Henry Wadsworth Longfellow

Date:

Write a poem about your closest friend. Don't worry about poetic form or start fretting if you haven't written a poem in years. Remember, this is your journal. It's for your eyes only (unless you choose to share it).

Date:

"All the words I use in my stories can be found in the dictionary—it's just a matter of arranging them into the right sentences."
– Somerset Maugham

Date:

When was the last time someone sang a song to you? Write about the experience. How did it make you feel? Why do you think they were doing it?

_____

_____

_____

_____

_____

_____

_____

_____

_____

_____

_____

_____

_____

_____

_____

_____

_____

Date:

"If you write one story, it may be bad; if you write a hundred, you have
the odds in your favor."
– Edgar Rice Burroughs

Date:

Do you think there are things that you cannot see (energy vibrations/spirits/ghosts)? Write about them. If you think the idea is silly, write about why you feel that way.

_____

_____

_____

_____

_____

_____

_____

_____

_____

_____

_____

_____

_____

_____

_____

_____

_____

Date:

"Don't be a writer; be writing."
by William Faulkner

Date:

What would be your ideal day? Describe it from dusk till dawn.
Let your imagination run wild, without thinking of any limits.

_____

_____

_____

_____

_____

_____

_____

_____

_____

_____

_____

_____

_____

_____

_____

_____

Date:

"The secret of it all is to write in the gush, the throb, the flood of the
moment–to put things down without deliberation–without worrying
about their style–without waiting for a fit time or place."
-Walt Whitman

Date:

Write about someone you miss immensely. When was the last time you saw them? What was that last time like?

_____

_____

_____

_____

_____

_____

_____

_____

_____

_____

_____

_____

_____

_____

_____

_____

_____

_____

Date:

"Let us answer a book of ink with a book of flesh and blood."
—Ralph Waldo Emerson

Date:

When was the last time you met a daily writing goal early? Why do you think you were successful on that day? How can you repeat that? Can you think of any factors that contributed to it (ex. a solid outline or peaceful environment or restful sleep the prior night, etc.)

_____

_____

_____

_____

_____

_____

_____

_____

_____

_____

_____

_____

_____

_____

_____

_____

Date:

"Being a good writer is 3% talent, 97% not being distracted by the Internet."
—Anonymous

Date:

What is your favorite book? Write a review about it as if you are writing an advertisement for it in a local newspaper.

Date:

If I waited for perfection... I would never write a word."
—Margaret Atwood

Date:

Write a tribute to a hero/heroine.

Date:

"A professional writer is an amateur who didn't quit."
—Richard Bach

Date:

What habits do you wish you would change/stop doing? Why?

_____

_____

_____

_____

_____

_____

_____

_____

_____

_____

_____

_____

_____

_____

_____

_____

_____

Date:

"And what, you ask, does writing teach us? First and foremost, it reminds us that we are alive and that it is a gift and a privilege, not a right."
—Ray Bradbury

Re-write the ending of the last movie you watched. How would you change things?

_____

_____

_____

_____

_____

_____

_____

_____

_____

_____

_____

_____

_____

_____

_____

_____

_____

Date:

"It is by sitting down to write every morning that one becomes
a writer."
—Gerald Brenan

Date:

What do you enjoy most about writing?
What do you enjoy least about it?

_____

_____

_____

_____

_____

_____

_____

_____

_____

_____

_____

_____

_____

_____

_____

_____

_____

Date:

"Writing is a delicious agony."
—Gwendolyn Brooks

_____

_____

_____

_____

_____

_____

_____

_____

_____

_____

_____

_____

_____

_____

_____

_____

Date:

If you could stretch tomorrow into a week, what would you do for the 'day'? Would you even sleep if you didn't feel tired? Think about the day feeling as long as a week and all you could accomplish. Imagine it in as much detail as you can.

Date:

"Good writing is rewriting."
—Truman Capote

_____

_____

_____

_____

_____

_____

_____

_____

_____

_____

_____

_____

_____

_____

_____

_____

_____

_____

_____

Date:

When do you feel most inspired to write?
What do you think leads to that inspiration? What are the
circumstances? What is the environment like?

_____

_____

_____

_____

_____

_____

_____

_____

_____

_____

_____

_____

_____

_____

_____

_____

Date:

"Outlining, researching, talking to people about what you're doing, none of that is writing. Writing is writing."
—E.L. Doctorow

Date:

When was the last time you felt out of place (in a crowd/room/meeting)? Write about the experience.
What made you feel out of place? Have you felt that way before?

_____

_____

_____

_____

_____

_____

_____

_____

_____

_____

_____

_____

_____

_____

_____

_____

_____

_____

Date:

"To survive, you must tell stories."
—Umberto Eco

_____

_____

_____

_____

_____

_____

_____

_____

_____

_____

_____

_____

_____

_____

_____

_____

_____

Date:

I want the world to know that…………

"Creative writers are always greater than the causes that they represent."
—E. M. Forster

Date:

If you could create the ideal writing space, what would it be? Describe it.

_____

_____

_____

_____

_____

_____

_____

_____

_____

_____

_____

_____

_____

_____

_____

_____

_____

_____

Date:

"Love is the only energy I've ever used as a writer. I've never written out of anger, although anger has informed love."
—Athol Fugard

Date:

What one thing do you long to do?

Date:

"The Six Golden Rules of Writing: Read, read, read, and write, write, write."
—Ernest Gaines

Date:

Do you have a recurrent dream? Or recurrent theme when dreaming (i.e. falling/being chased)? Describe it in as much detail as you can. To recall specifics, try to think about the last time you had this dream.

_____

_____

_____

_____

_____

_____

_____

_____

_____

_____

_____

_____

_____

_____

_____

_____

_____

_____

Date:

"Be courageous and try to write in a way that scares you a little."
—Holly Gerth

_____

_____

_____

_____

_____

_____

_____

_____

_____

_____

_____

_____

_____

_____

_____

_____

_____

Date:

When was your last long road trip? Where did you go? Why? If you haven't been on one, imagine one that you'd like to take.

_____

_____

_____

_____

_____

_____

_____

_____

_____

_____

_____

_____

_____

_____

_____

_____

_____

Date:

"The most beautiful things are those that madness prompts and reason writes."
—Andre Gide

Date:

What does fall time (autumn) make you think of? What sights, sounds, smells does it trigger?

_____

_____

_____

_____

_____

_____

_____

_____

_____

_____

_____

_____

_____

_____

_____

_____

_____

Date:

"Writers live twice."
—Natalie Goldberg

Date:

Think of a strong emotion (the first that comes to mind). Can you recall two different memories where you felt that emotion? Describe them both. How were the events different/alike?

_____

_____

_____

_____

_____

_____

_____

_____

_____

_____

_____

_____

_____

_____

_____

_____

_____

_____

Date:

"Being a writer requires an intoxication with language."
—Jim Harrison

_____

_____

_____

_____

_____

_____

_____

_____

_____

_____

_____

_____

_____

_____

_____

_____

_____

_____

Date:

What do you want to write about more than anything else? What type of genre? In what style and tone? If you are unsure, think about a piece of writing / author / book that embodies what you would like to write like. Describe it.

_____

_____

_____

_____

_____

_____

_____

_____

_____

_____

_____

_____

_____

_____

_____

_____

_____

_____

Date:

"Serious writers write, inspired or not. Over time they discover that routine is a better friend than inspiration."
—Ralph Keyes

Date:

Is there an event in your life that angered you the most? Why? Has the anger subsided or amplified over time?

Date:

"Being a writer means taking the leap from listening to saying, "'Listen to me."
—Jhumpa Lahiri

Date:

Is there any single experience that has most shaped who you are in your life? Describe it in detail.

_____

_____

_____

_____

_____

_____

_____

_____

_____

_____

_____

_____

_____

_____

_____

_____

_____

_____

Date:

"Almost all good writing begins with terrible first efforts. You need to start somewhere."
—Anne Lamott

Date:

Have you ever had a writing session where everything was just flowing? There was little thought, just a fluid, easy flow of words? Write about that time. What were you writing about?

_____

_____

_____

_____

_____

_____

_____

_____

_____

_____

_____

_____

_____

_____

_____

_____

Date:

"Writing—the art of communicating thoughts to the mind, through the eye—is the great invention of the world."
—Abraham Lincoln

Date:

Is there anyone you would not want to read your writing? This can be someone you know, admire, or even despise.

Date:

"The secret of good writing is telling the truth."
—Gordon Lish

Date:

They say the pen is mightier than the sword. Do you agree with this?

_____

_____

_____

_____

_____

_____

_____

_____

_____

_____

_____

_____

_____

_____

_____

_____

_____

Date:

"Until you know who you are you can't write."
—Salman Rushdie

_____

_____

_____

_____

_____

_____

_____

_____

_____

_____

_____

_____

_____

_____

_____

_____

Date:

Think of an item you cherished in childhood. Describe it in detail.
When did you get it? Why did you like it so much?

_____

_____

_____

_____

_____

_____

_____

_____

_____

_____

_____

_____

_____

_____

_____

_____

_____

_____

Date:

"I start with a question. Then try to answer it."
—Mary Lee Settle

Do you have a place that inspires your writing or that inspires you in general? Describe it.

_____

_____

_____

_____

_____

_____

_____

_____

_____

_____

_____

_____

_____

_____

_____

_____

_____

Date:

"Art is not a handicraft, it is the transmission of feeling the artist has experienced."
—Leo Tolstoy

Date:

If you could plan the perfect writing getaway/retreat, what would it be like? Where would it be?

_____

_____

_____

_____

_____

_____

_____

_____

_____

_____

_____

_____

_____

_____

_____

_____

_____

_____

_____

Date:

"Art is the symbol of the two noblest human efforts: to construct and to refrain from deconstruction."
—Evelyn Waugh

Date:

What is the best piece you've ever written? This could even be a poem
or story or article from long ago. Why do you feel it is the best?

_____

_____

_____

_____

_____

_____

_____

_____

_____

_____

_____

_____

_____

_____

_____

_____

_____

Date:

"If you do not tell the truth about yourself you cannot tell it about other people."
—Virginia Woolf

Date:

If you could, would you trade places with someone else's life? Who?
Why?

Date:

"The artist must possess the courageous soul that dares and defies."
—Kate Chopin

Date:

Think of an event where you felt a strong spiritual/other-worldly energy (something you could not see or touch) that was present. What was happening? How did you feel? Describe the event in detail. Did it change the way you view life in any way?

_____

_____

_____

_____

_____

_____

_____

_____

_____

_____

_____

_____

_____

_____

_____

_____

_____

Date:

"To gain your own voice, you have to forget about having it heard."
—Allen Ginsberg

Date:

Describe the most significant epiphany of your life. Where were you?
What lead to it? What did you do after? How did it change your life?

_____

_____

_____

_____

_____

_____

_____

_____

_____

_____

_____

_____

_____

_____

_____

_____

_____

_____

Date:

"Do not wait to strike till the iron is hot; but make it hot by striking."
—William B. Sprague

Date:

Is there are decision you are grappling to make in your life right now?
What is it? What are you weighing up to make that decision?

_____

_____

_____

_____

_____

_____

_____

_____

_____

_____

_____

_____

_____

_____

_____

_____

_____

Date:

"Inspiration is a guest that does not willingly visit the lazy."
—Pyotr Tchaikovsky

Date:

Who is the one person you turn to for most advice? Why?

_____

_____

_____

_____

_____

_____

_____

_____

_____

_____

_____

_____

_____

_____

_____

_____

_____

Date:

Have you ever read a poem or article that moved you deeply? What was it? How did it move you?

_____

_____

_____

_____

_____

_____

_____

_____

_____

_____

_____

_____

_____

_____

_____

_____

_____

Printed in Poland
by Amazon Fulfillment
Poland Sp. z o.o., Wrocław